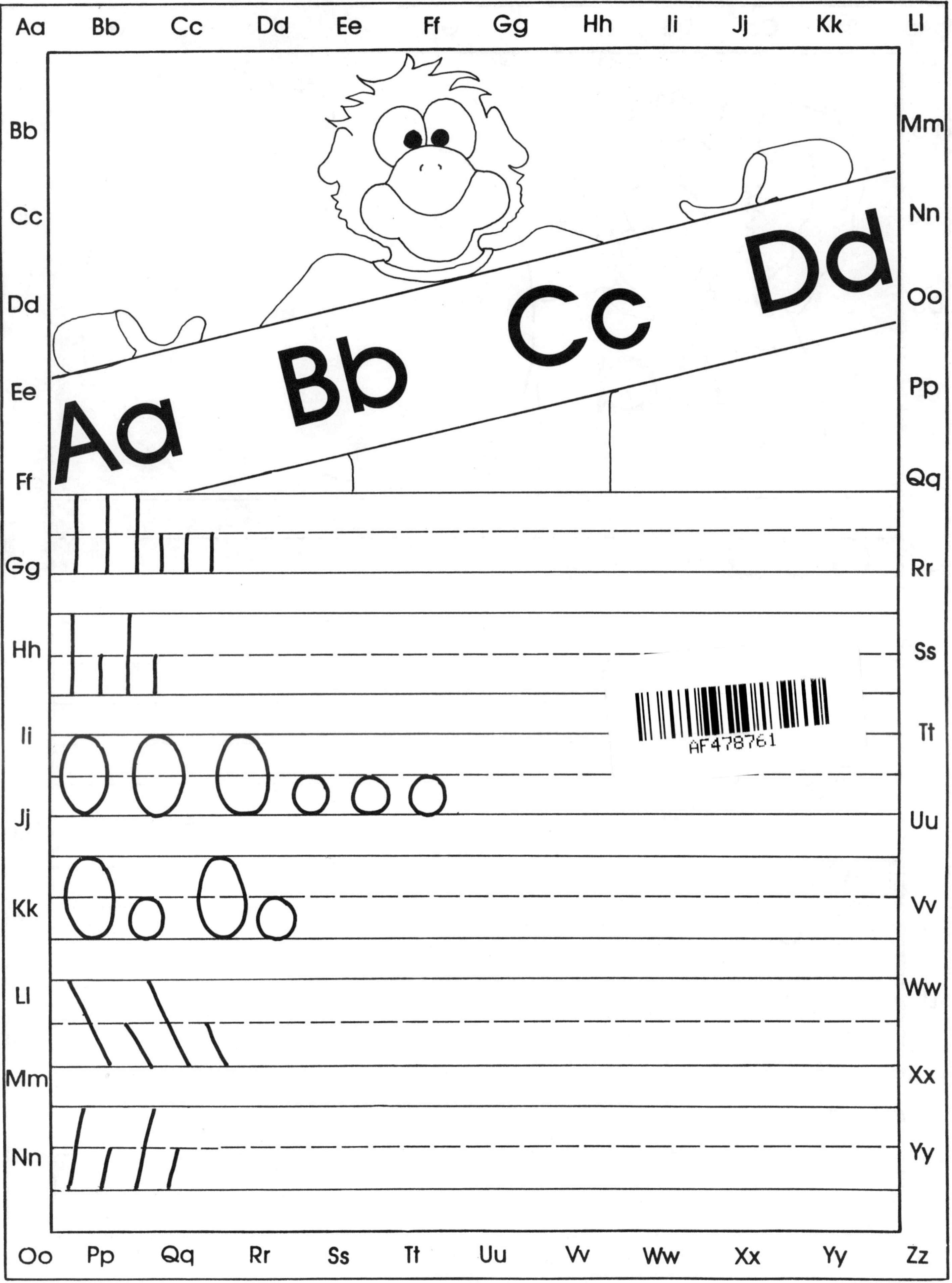

©1984 by EVAN-MOOR CORP.

Monkey Manuscript

©1984 by EVAN-MOOR CORP.

2

Monkey Manuscript

©1984 by EVAN-MOOR CORP.

Monkey Manuscript

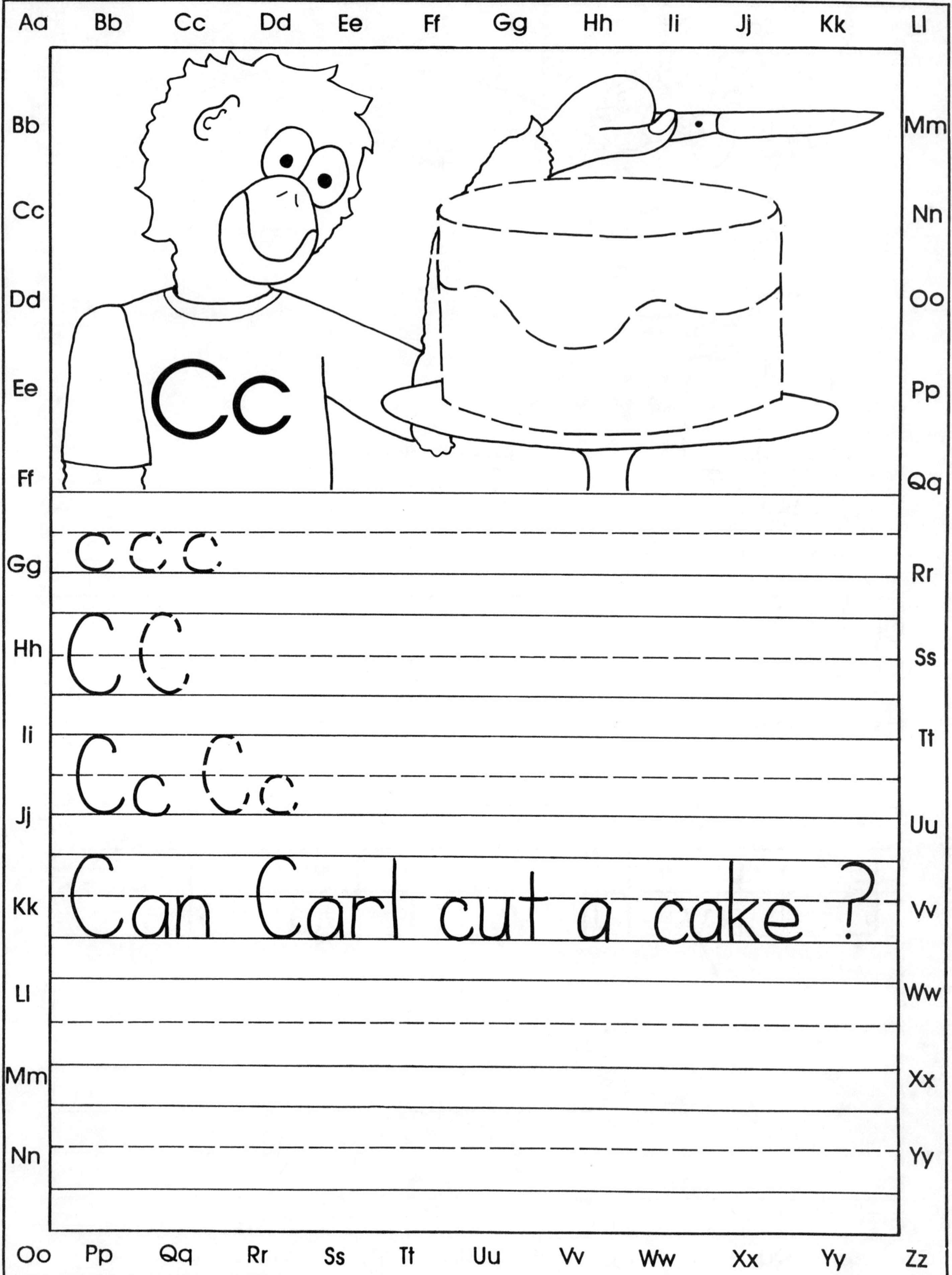

©1984 by EVAN-MOOR CORP.

4

Monkey Manuscript

d d d

D D

Dd Dd

Dan drew a dinosaur.

©1984 by EVAN-MOOR CORP.

Monkey Manuscript

©1984 by EVAN-MOOR CORP.

6

Monkey Manuscript

©1984 by EVAN-MOOR CORP.

Monkey Manuscript

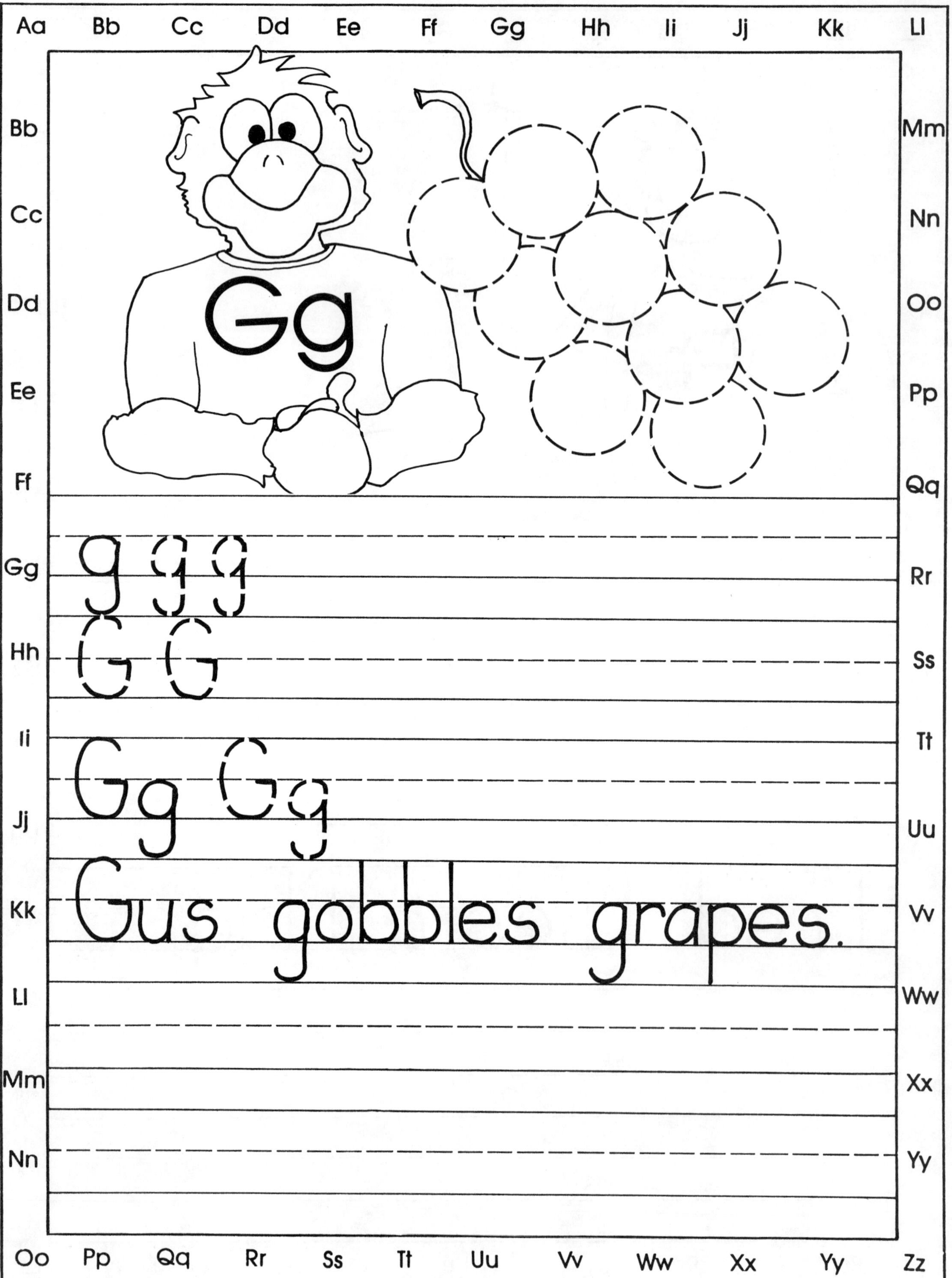

©1984 by EVAN-MOOR CORP.

8

Monkey Manuscript

©1984 by EVAN-MOOR CORP.

Monkey Manuscript

Bb
Cc
Dd
Ee
Ff
Gg
Hh
Ii
Jj
Kk
Ll
Mm
Nn

Mm
Nn
Oo
Pp
Qq
Rr
Ss
Tt
Uu
Vv
Ww
Xx
Yy

©1984 by EVAN-MOOR CORP.

Monkey Manuscript

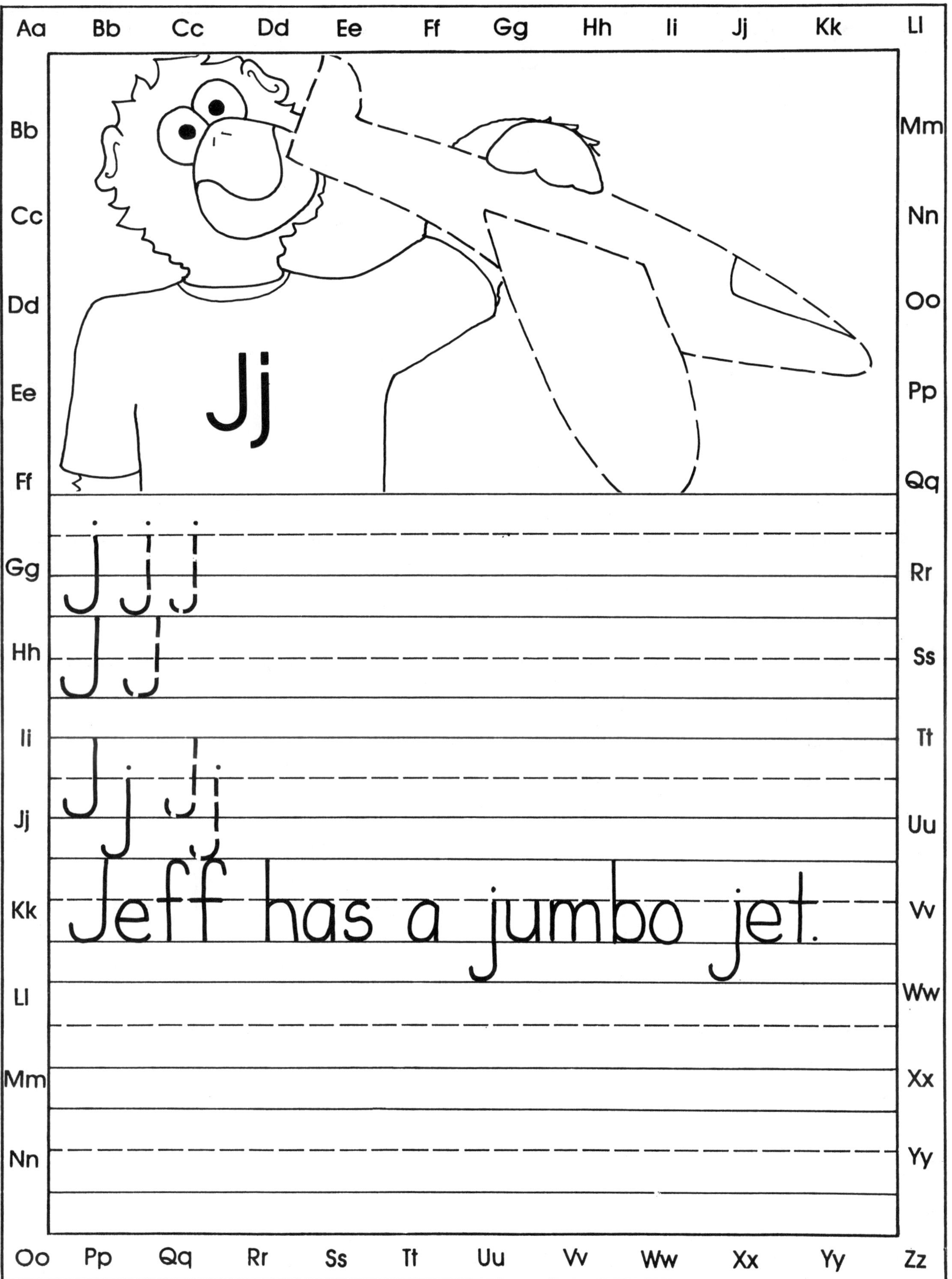

J J J
J J
J j j j
Jeff has a jumbo jet.

©1984 by EVAN-MOOR CORP.

Monkey Manuscript

K K K

K K K

K K K

Kris kissed her kitten.

©1984 by EVAN-MOOR CORP.

Monkey Manuscript

©1984 by EVAN-MOOR CORP.

Monkey Manuscript

©1984 by EVAN-MOOR CORP.

14

Monkey Manuscript

©1984 by EVAN-MOOR CORP.

Monkey Manuscript

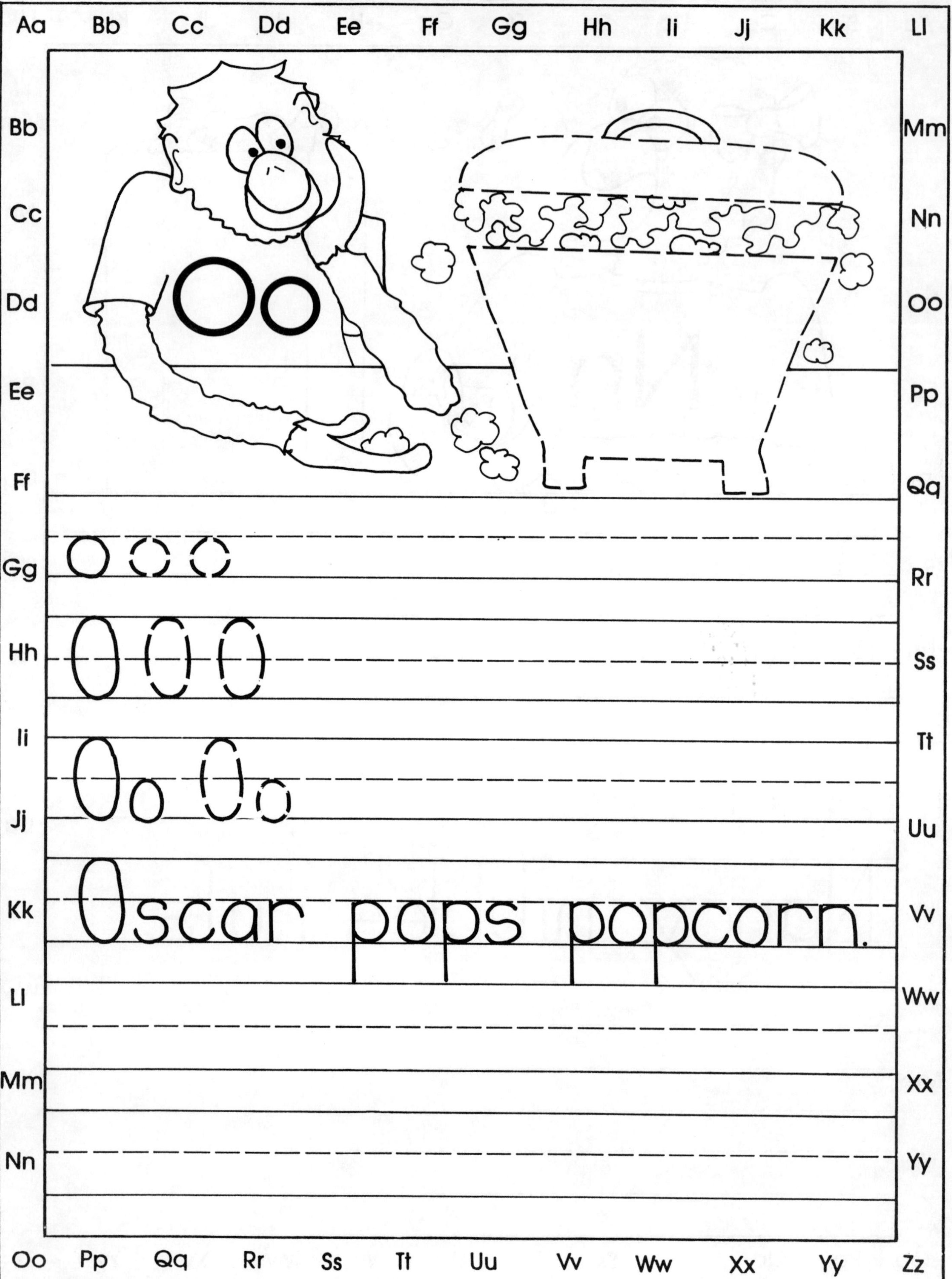

Oscar pops popcorn.

©1984 by EVAN-MOOR CORP.

16

Monkey Manuscript

p p p
P P

P p P p

Pam picked a present.

©1984 by EVAN-MOOR CORP.   17   Monkey Manuscript

Aa Bb Cc Dd Ee Ff Gg Hh Ii Jj Kk Ll

Bb Cc Dd Ee Ff Gg Hh Ii Jj Kk Ll Mm Nn

Mm Nn Oo Pp Qq Rr Ss Tt Uu Vv Ww Xx Yy

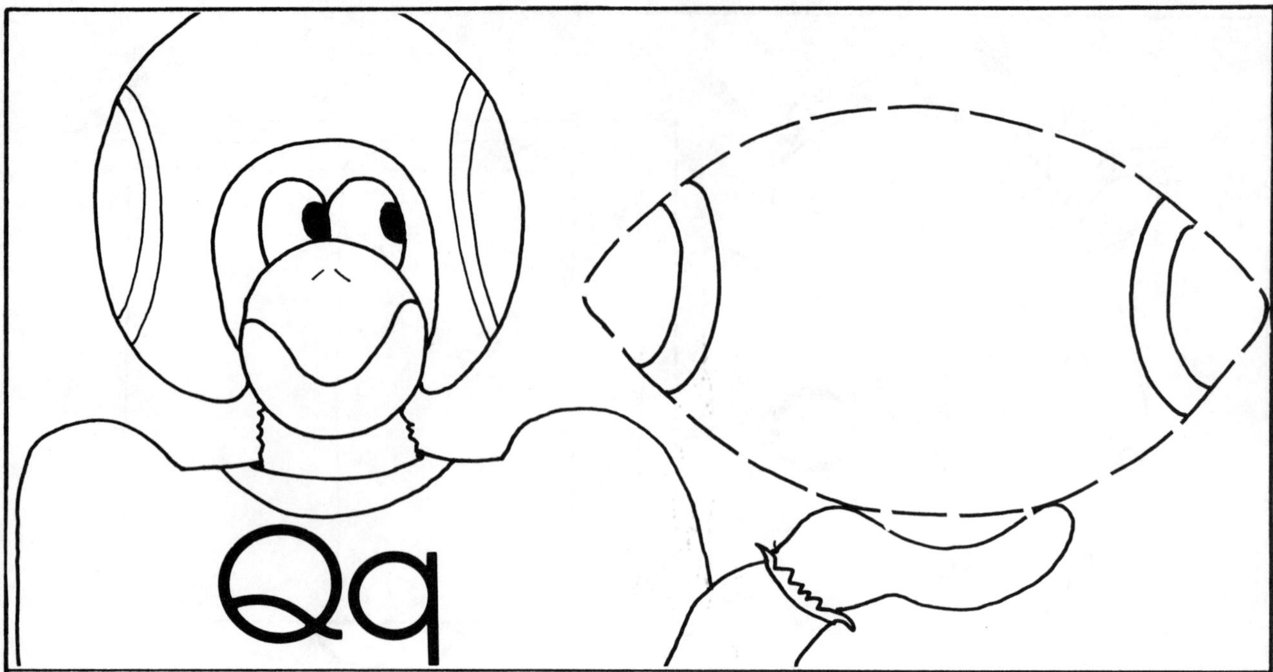

q q q

Q Q

Qq Qq

Quincy is quick.

Oo Pp Qq Rr Ss Tt Uu Vv Ww Xx Yy Zz

©1984 by EVAN-MOOR CORP.

©1984 by EVAN-MOOR CORP.

Monkey Manuscript

©1984 by EVAN-MOOR CORP.

Monkey Manuscript

Tom tips the truck.

©1984 by EVAN-MOOR CORP.

Monkey Manuscript

Aa Bb Cc Dd Ee Ff Gg Hh Ii Jj Kk Ll
Bb Mm
Cc Nn
Dd Oo
Ee Pp
Ff Qq
Gg Rr
Hh Ss
Ii Tt
Jj Uu
Kk Vv
Ll Ww
Mm Xx
Nn Yy
Oo Pp Qq Rr Ss Tt Uu Vv Ww Xx Yy Zz

Uu
U U U
U U
Uu Uu
Uri put up an umbrella.

©1984 by EVAN-MOOR CORP.

Monkey Manuscript

Ww
W W W
W W
Ww Ww
Willie works on wagons.

©1984 by EVAN-MOOR CORP.

25

Monkey Manuscript

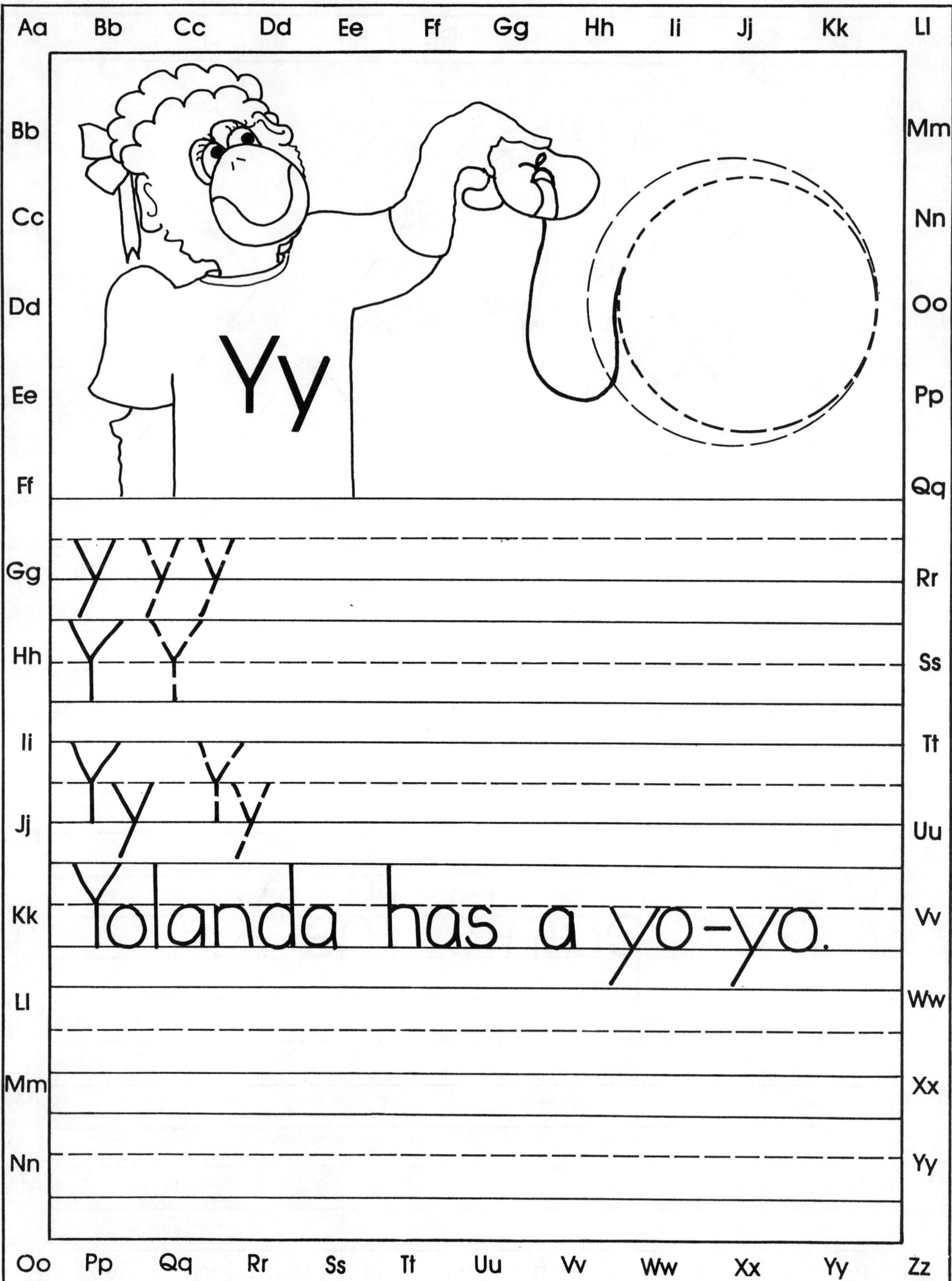

©1984 by EVAN-MOOR CORP.

26

Monkey Manuscript

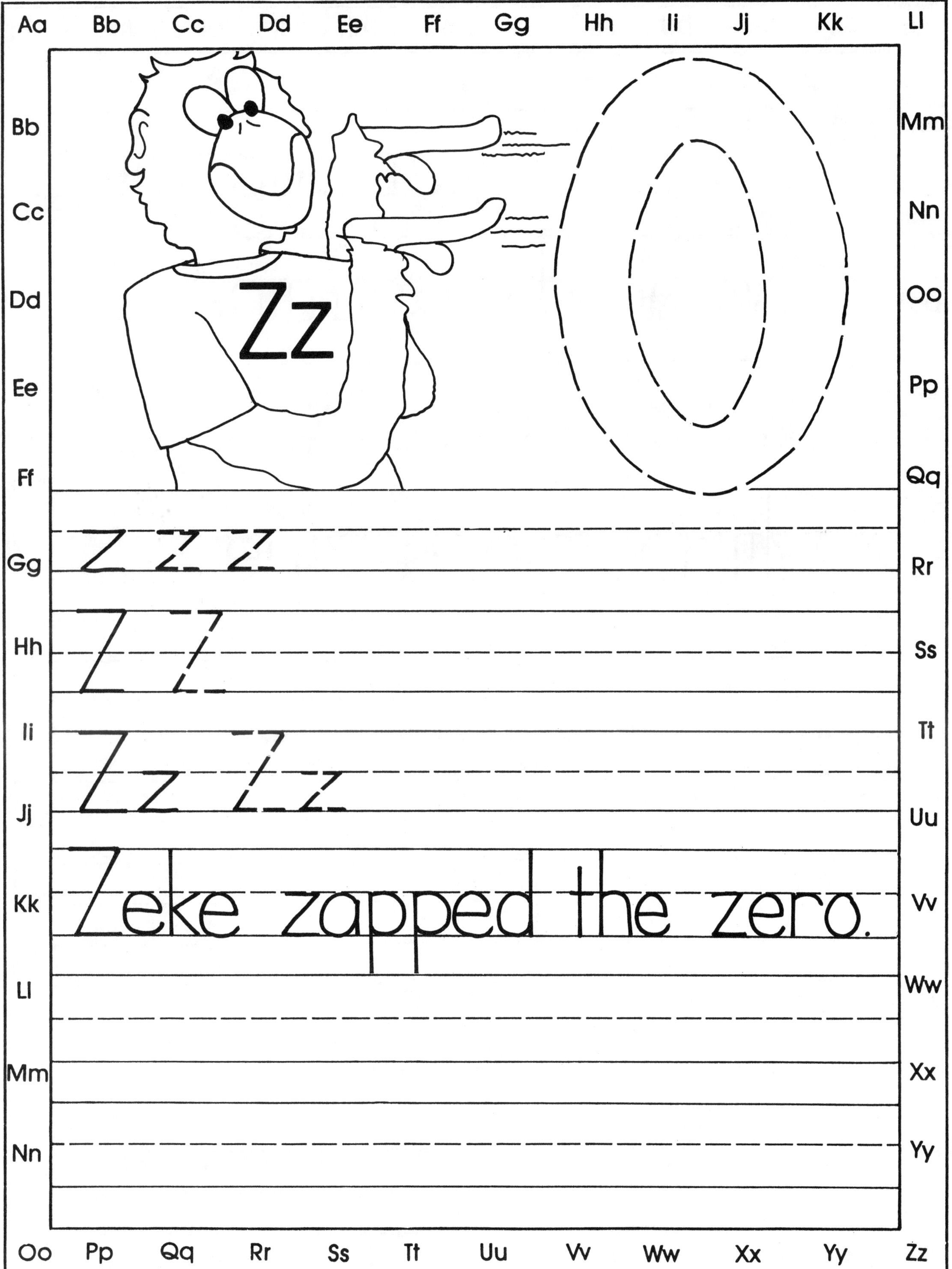

©1984 by EVAN-MOOR CORP.

27

Monkey Manuscript

©1984 by EVAN-MOOR CORP.

28

Monkey Manuscript

©1984 by EVAN-MOOR CORP.

Monkey Manuscript

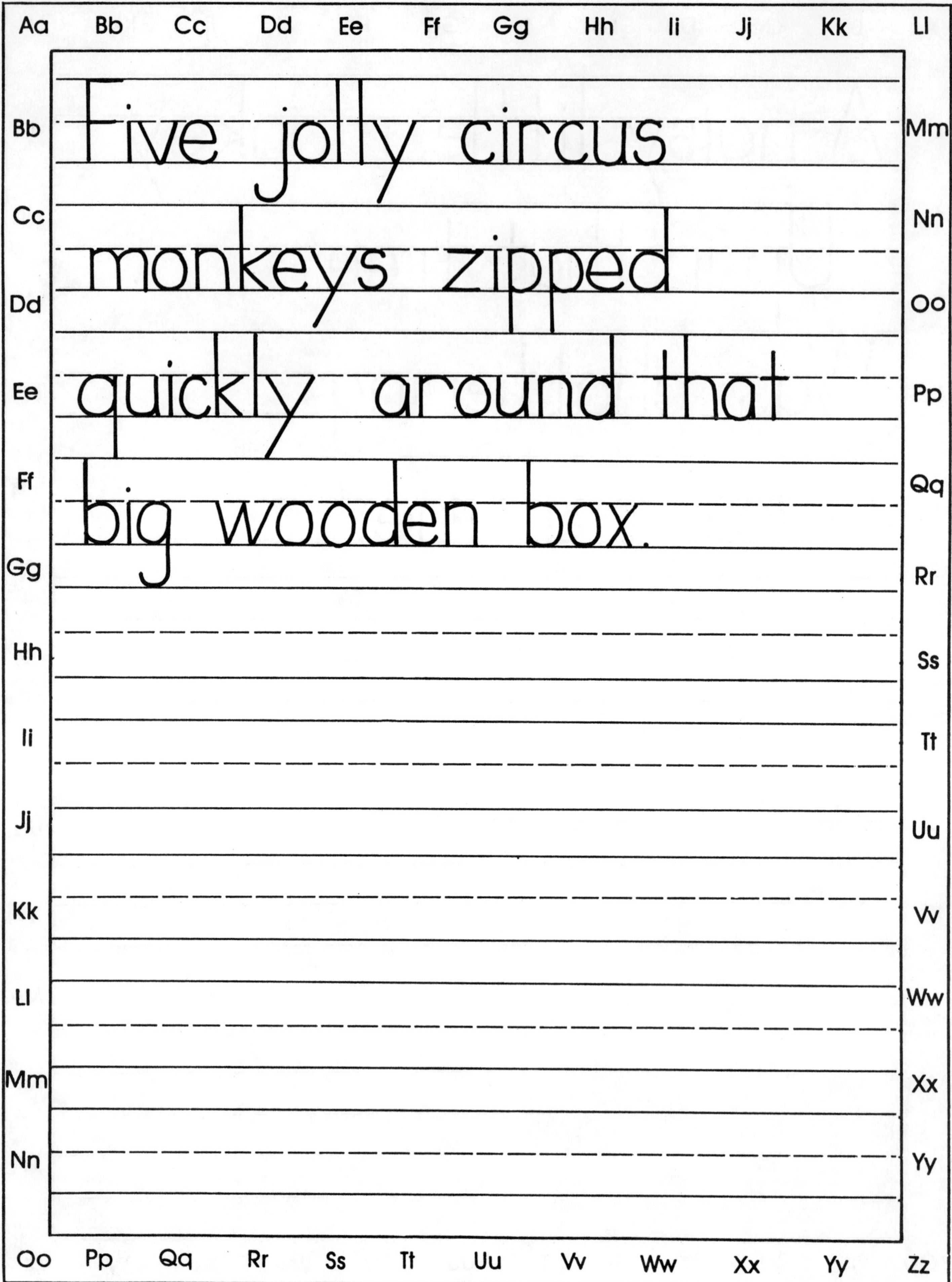

©1984 by EVAN-MOOR CORP.

Monkey Manuscript

Aa Bb Cc Dd Ee Ff Gg Hh Ii Jj Kk Ll
Bb Cc Dd Ee Ff Gg Hh Ii Jj Kk Ll Mm Nn Oo Pp Qq Rr Ss Tt Uu Vv Ww Xx Yy
Oo Pp Qq Rr Ss Tt Uu Vv Ww Xx Yy Zz

©1984 by EVAN-MOOR CORP.

Monkey Manuscript

Handwriting Award

©1984 by EVAN-MOOR CORP.

32

Monkey Manuscript